WHY MEN ARE CLUELESS

BY
JAN KING

Illustrated by
JERRY KING

C C C   P U B L I C A T I O N S

Published by

CCC Publications
1111 Rancho Conejo Blvd.
Suites 411 & 412
Newbury Park, CA 91320

Manufactured in the United States of America

Cover ©1995 CCC Publications

Interior illustrations ©1995 CCC Publications

Cover & interior art by Jerry King

Cover/Interior production by Oasis Graphics

ISBN: 0-918259-83-5

If your local U.S. bookstore is out of stock, copies of this book may be obtained by mailing check or money order for $4.99 per book (plus $2.50 to cover postage and handling) to: CCC Publications; 111 Rancho Conejo Blvd.; Suites 411 & 412; Newbury Park, CA 91320

Pre-publication Edition – 5/95

This book is dedicated with much love to my dear friends
Paul and Margaret Herrman

INTRODUCTION

How many times have you been arguing with your partner and it suddenly dawns on you that he has absolutely NO IDEA what you're talking about or what you're feeling? You're trying to reason with a man who is totally "clueless." When this happens, you usually feel like banging your head against the wall in utter frustration.

Well, the good news is that you won't have to resort to bashing your head anymore. You can resort to Male-Bashing instead by reading "Why Men Are Clueless." This little book illustrates many of the situations that have driven you nuts over the years and provides you with those much-needed therapeutic laughs. Too bad it isn't "required reading" for every man on the planet.

Why is it that men have the WORLD'S WORST timing when it comes to having sex.

Why do men always RUIN the moment of passion by saying something totally clueless?

Why can't men understand that when you have the flu with a 103° temperature, you're not exactly ready for a wild roll in the hay?

Why do macho-men always think that the harder they go at it, the more you're going to love it?

Why is it that after a knock-down, drag-out fight, men always think that having sex will make everything all right again?

Why will men NEVER admit
they're getting fat?

Why does a man always want to take your picture when you look your absolute WORST? Then, after it's developed, he goes around showing it to EVERYBODY.

Why do men always reveal secrets about you in front of a bunch of your friends?

Why don't guys realize that no woman wants to make love to a man who is smelly, unshaven, and who hasn't brushed his teeth in three days?

Why do all men forget what table manners are the second they get married?

When will guys ever learn that bragging about past conquests is strictly "high school" behavior and one of the biggest turn-offs on Earth?

Why do men refuse to open doors
for a woman?

Why don't men have a clue about
how to dress their kids?

Why do men walk AHEAD of you or BEHIND you, but never WITH you?

Why don't men have a clue about what clothes go together?

Why don't men appreciate the kind of work it takes a woman to doll herself up for her man?

Why don't men have a clue as to what is an appropriate gift for his wife's birthday?

Why is it that a man is unable to muster up even an ounce of sympathy for his sick wife?

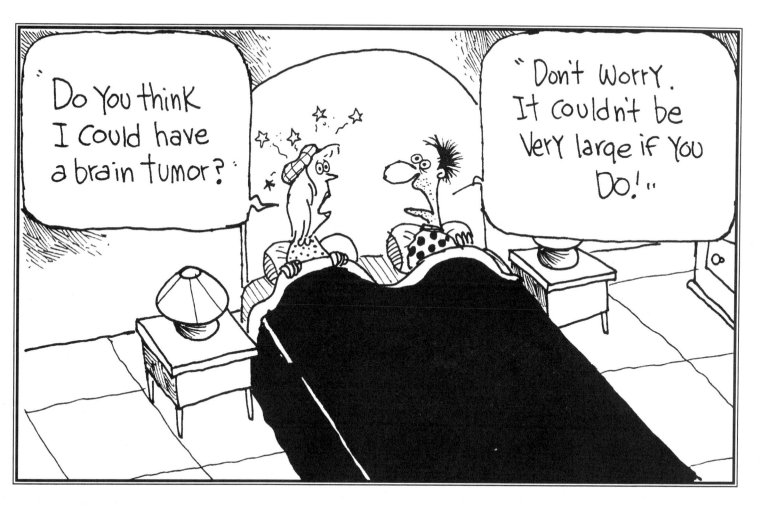

Why does a man go all throughout dinner without saying a word to you. However, when the waitress comes over to the table, he's suddenly "Mr. Bubbly Personality?"

Why can't men even LIE convincingly?

Why does a guy think it's okay for him to make an ass out of himself at a party, but YOU aren't allowed to even tell a joke?

Why do clueless men promote promiscuity in their sons but demand that their daughters behave like Nuns?

Why can't a man ever say anything nice about the dinner you slaved over all day?

Why don't men understand that during the last three months of pregnancy your body has changed dramatically?

Why don't men realize that after delivering a 8 lb. baby, you're not quite ready to git it on – in this century, anyway.

Why can't a man appreciate the hours of work you put into a dinner party for his boss so HE will look great?

"Honey, can you pick up the kids at my sister's?"
"Can't you see I'm exhausted? Entertaining my Boss has been a very draining experience for me!"

Why is it that men define a romantic movie as "anything X-Rated"?

Why can't men understand that making love is something special between two people who care for each other and not something to be quickly squeezed in between dinner and a movie?

Why can't men face that fact that women are EQUAL to them and not inferior beings to be bossed around?

Why must men live their lives according to what their friends think?

Titles By CCC PUBLICATIONS

Retail $4.99
POSITIVELY PREGNANT
SIGNS YOUR SEX LIFE IS DEAD
WHY MEN DON'T HAVE A CLUE
40 AND HOLDING YOUR OWN
CAN SEX IMPROVE YOUR GOLF?
THE COMPLETE BOOGER BOOK
THINGS YOU CAN DO WITH A USELESS MAN
FLYING FUNNIES
MARITAL BLISS & OXYMORONS
THE VERY VERY SEXY ADULT
   DOT-TO-DOT BOOK
THE DEFINITIVE FART BOOK
THE COMPLETE WIMP'S GUIDE TO SEX
THE CAT OWNER'S SHAPE UP MANUAL
PMS CRAZED: TOUCH ME AND I'LL KILL YOU!
RETIRED: LET THE GAMES BEGIN
MALE BASHING: WOMEN'S FAVORITE PASTIME
THE OFFICE FROM HELL
FOOD & SEX
FITNESS FANATICS
YOUNGER MEN ARE BETTER THAN RETIN-A
BUT OSSIFER, IT'S NOT MY FAULT

Retail $4.95
1001 WAYS TO PROCRASTINATE
THE WORLD'S GREATEST PUT-DOWN LINES
HORMONES FROM HELL II

SHARING THE ROAD WITH IDIOTS
THE GREATEST ANSWERING MACHINE
   MESSAGES OF ALL TIME
WHAT DO WE DO NOW?? (A Guide For New
   Parents)
HOW TO TALK YOU WAY OUT OF A TRAFFIC
   TICKET
THE BOTTOM HALF (How To Spot Incompetent
   Professionals)
LIFE'S MOST EMBARRASSING MOMENTS
HOW TO ENTERTAIN PEOPLE YOU HATE
YOUR GUIDE TO CORPORATE SURVIVAL
THE SUPERIOR PERSON'S GUIDE TO
   EVERYDAY IRRITATIONS
GIFTING RIGHT

Retail $5.95
50 WAYS TO HUSTLE YOUR FRIENDS ($5.99)
HORMONES FROM HELL
HUSBANDS FROM HELL
KILLER BRAS & Other Hazards Of The 50's
IT'S BETTER TO BE OVER THE HILL THAN
   UNDER IT
HOW TO REALLY PARTY!!!
WORK SUCKS!
THE PEOPLE WATCHER'S FIRLD GUIDE
THE UNOFFICIAL WOMEN'S DIVORCE GUIDE
THE ABSOLUTE LAST CHANCE DIET BOOK

FOR MEN ONLY (How To Survive Marriage)
THE UGLY TRUTH ABOUT MEN
NEVER A DULL CARD
RED HOT MONOGAMY
   (In Just 60 Seconds A Day) ($6.95)

Retail $3.95
YOU KNOW YOU'RE AN OLD FART WHEN...
NO HANG-UPS
NO HANG-UPS II
NO HANG-UPS III
GETTING EVEN WITH THE ANSWERING
   MACHINE
HOW TO SUCCEED IN SINGLES BARS
HOW TO GET EVEN WITH YOUR EXES
TOTALLY OUTRAGEOUS BUMPER-SNICKERS
   ($2.95)

NO HANG-UPS – CASSETTES Retail $4.98

Vol. I:	GENERAL MESSAGES	(Female)
Vol. I:	GENERAL MESSAGES	(Male)
Vol. II:	BUSINESS MESSAGES	(Female)
Vol. II:	BUSINESS MESSAGES	(Male)
Vol. III:	'R' RATED MESSAGES	(Female)
Vol. III:	'R' RATED MESSAGES	(Male)
Vol. IV:	SOUND EFFECTS ONLY	
Vol. V:	CELEBRI-TEASE	